In *Total Recall,* Samantha Giles has a story ~~of fathers and abuse~~ to tell, but finds only a vortex in the telling. "I am trying to tell you" she writes—it is easy to believe how anguish inevitably comes spurting out of the wasteland of our subconscious. "I do want to tell you," she writes—it is difficult to recognise how often we substitute exposition for trauma. "I really do want to try to tell you everything,"—in a mobius strip of movie madness, lyric fragment and sub/ob-jective statement of fact, Giles diligently jigsaws her splintered memory into the misleadingly elegant frames of reality in order to present it—at least partially—to the paternal forces of world, to the law, even to herself. Indeed, *Total Recall* is significant, not for fixating on the moment of trauma itself, but for living within the kind of marked restlessness and intense isolation that comes with bearing an impossible burden of proof. Finding a hellish pleasure in the slow chiseling away of the false from the real, the real from the false, Giles peels our eyelids back with no hope of looking away from a nameless core. Don't blink.

Trisha Low

Policing of memory is a serious enterprise historically and always. Memory is forever at risk of becoming the disappeared. Social, political, and personal accusations of fake news, false facts, erased data, and implanted memories, are just a few of the many ways human beings like to terrorize each other in order to have a go at "truth" when truth is inconvenient and or damning. Samantha Giles's *Total Recall* is so singularly stunning and uncategorizable that I can only speak to its power in terms of how she uses language to pull the reader into a very particular form of witnessing—one of simultaneously wanting to tune the ugly out and one of wanting to protect, contain, and make a safe space for trauma. *Total Recall* is giving us a magnificent account of a self who, for better or for worse, knows that "we are in this together, we are in this together, we are in this together."

Kim Rosenfield

SAMANTHA GILES

TOTAL RECALL

KRUPSKAYA • 2018

and then you're someone you are not,
and Junction City ain't the spot,
remember Mrs. Lot
and when she turned around?

- Stephen Trask

Remorse - is Memory - awake -
Her Parties all astir -

- Emily Dickinson

You tell me what you think happened
and I'll tell you where you're wrong.

- My father

TOTAL RECALL

In the 1990 movie *Total Recall*, a man is haunted by a recurring dream about a journey to Mars. The movie is set during a hyper-technological imagined future.

During the same year that the film was released in theaters, a woman, along with the support of her grandmother and uncle, privately confronted her father for having had a sexual relationship with her throughout her childhood.

Her father denied her allegations, stating that surely someone in the household would have been aware of his behavior at the time and no one was. He claimed that the family dog would have barked due to the commotion elicited by his actions, making others in the household aware of their sexual relationship. But because the family dog did not bark, according to the father, the daughter's story was clearly false.

The man's dreams of Mars are all consuming. They seem more real to him than his real life. He wakes up in a fever after having had a very realistic dream of kissing a woman who is not his wife on what appears to be a fairly-hospitable-to-humans version of Mars.

Over breakfast, the man suggests somewhat insistently to his wife they take a vacation to the distant planet, which his wife immediately dismisses. There are political difficulties in the region I think. It's just not attractive to her as a vacation spot. She uses the promise of sex to distract him.

A year after the small family confrontation and the father's refusal, the daughter's mother published an anonymous first-person account of the encounter in a journal whose focus was the false accusation of child sexual abuse.

The mother's article was circulated widely including to her daughter's workplace and without her daughter's consent.

On the way to his job as a construction worker the man sees an advertisement on the subway, on a kind of futuristic-for-the-time television screen right on the train. The ad is for ReKall, Inc., a facility that implants fake memories of ideal vacations.

The advertisement claims that implanting memories of a life is far less expensive than trying to experience the real thing.

I should probably say that the first time I ever heard the term "false memories" my father accused me of having them.

The daughter who had made the initial accusation claimed there were numerous inaccuracies in her mother's account, including the circumstances of the original accusation wherein the mother asserted that the daughter's "memories" had only resulted from her therapy sessions as an adult. The daughter, however, claimed she had never not remembered her father's actions.

Despite his wife's attempts to thwart his enthusiasm for Mars, the man remains undeterred. This unchecked desire for something so strangely familiar to him, so *real*, consumes him.

After gaining traction with the journal article, The False Memory Syndrome Foundation is formed by the mother and the father of the daughter who had confronted her father one year earlier.

The early membership and advisory board of the foundation consisted of parents who had been accused of sexually abusing their now-adult children but it rapidly expanded to include professionals with expertise in the area of memory.

The website for the Foundation now lists over a hundred pages of credentialed supporters, even those who are now deceased. It's hard not to notice that the tone of the biographies of the supporters is overwhelmingly paternal.

The first time I ever heard the term "false memories" was at a dinner with my parents and my boyfriend. I think this was the first time I heard it anyway.

That is, I think I remember the phrase making a linguistic impression.

The man still really wants to get to Mars but he doesn't have the money and there's the problem of his wife.

So, against the advice of his co-worker, and without informing his wife of the plan, the man makes an appointment with ReKall, Inc. While there, he orders a special package that will implant memories of an adventure vacation where the man will inhabit the identity of a secret agent. He will be able to, in his implanted experience, kiss a woman who looks exactly like the one from his dream.

While he is surprised to see her face in the portfolio of options, he doesn't hesitate to select her.

The conversation at dinner with my parents was probably tense before the term "false memory" had even come up.

We were having dinner together after having intentionally not seen or talked to each other for at least a year and a half. The "we" here being my mother and father, my boyfriend and I. I think I'm remembering this right.

We were trying to make some of the same gestures at togetherness that we had made before, but there was this underlying and unspoken tension for having not been together for a while. My father and I had had a sort of fight about a year and a half before this dinner and I hadn't made the gestures I was expected to make in response to this sort of fight and so there was a year and a half gap and then there was this dinner.

The False Memory Syndrome movement's official literature describes its so-called "syndrome" as a "condition in which a person's identity and interpersonal relationships are centered around a memory of traumatic experience which is objectively false but in which the person strangely believes."

Back in the Rekall office something goes wrong with the memory implantation.

Inducing memory loss has long been a CIA obsession. The initial objectives included closing the minds of agents—in case they were captured—and making sure enemies who were interrogated wouldn't remember they'd been questioned.

So it's not entirely surprising to find that one of the early advisors of the False Memory Syndrome Foundation was noted for having worked for the CIA in these kind of techniques.

Before the sort of fight we had had about a year and a half before the dinner, it's probably fair to say that I had always made the right kind of gestures concerning my father. The kind of gestures that didn't put up a fight.

It's mostly accurate to say that the memory of my father at the dinner table that night is one of a man who had always felt he was on top of things, but who now felt there were things he was not on top of, and he needed to make some gestures to haul himself back up to the top of things.

At the dinner my father started reminiscing about his own life. I think I remember it as he was talking about his life as a series of instances where he had successfully made the gestures of hauling himself up.

He retold some of his memories that I had heard before—that is, I remembered hearing these memories of his all my life—but he told them at dinner that night a little differently.

In the movie the something wrong with the implantation is called a "schizoid embolism." It seems like a pretty serious thing to have go wrong in the process of memory implantation. The workers at the Rekall office are surprised by the man's reaction to this difficulty in implantation.

I should say that he specifically directed the sharing of these memories at my boyfriend, not to me. In this story I am sitting next to my boyfriend at my parents' very small dinner table which had replaced the one they had had when I was a child, having been raised in the same apartment in which we were now having this dinner.

False Memory Syndrome activists are driven to get those who recall abuse in therapy to recant their "objectively false" recollections. There is a lot of conversation on their website about what corroborates a *true* memory. I think there are the words "proof of genital bruising by a trusted medical professional."

I remember my father telling a lot of stories, one right after the other, that night. I had heard a version of all of these memories before, but I remembered them differently than my father was telling them that night, the night I first remember hearing the phrase "false memories."

It seemed like in the versions he was telling that night he was making the character in the stories, that is himself, less culpable and more heroic than I had remembered in previous versions of the same stories.

The character in the stories that night had successfully hauled himself up by the end of each episode. Hauled himself all the way to the top.

The schizoid embolism causes the man who wants to go to Mars to shout and thrash about in the chair, violently, struggling to break the straps that hold him down.

For example, while explaining how successful he was during his time in prison as a younger man, my father said the reason he had gone to prison was because he legitimately bought a car from some rich kid who didn't have permission to sell his dad's car. He made a lot of gestures of scorn for this rich kid for whom he'd taken the fall.

But in another version of that story not told on that night, I remember hearing or being told that he was convicted of car theft, statutory rape, and transporting a minor across state lines. Possibly there were two separate stints in prison: one for the car and one for the rape. Or maybe he had burgled houses with my uncle, canceling out the time spent for stealing a car. And I think there was also a version where it was kidnapping and transporting a minor and rape but no theft.

I don't have any proof of what actually happened that sent him to prison or for how many times he was there. These are all just things I remember hearing.

The schizoid embolism makes the man act like a different person or maybe even not a person at all. A caged animal suddenly realizing that the cage is trying to kill him and he needs desperately to break it.

False memory syndrome advocates claim: "Many describe a sense of relief and comfort with their decision that their memories were false and a sense of well-being that they missed while entrenched in the memory recovery process."

My father's memory of his father, my grandfather, beating my father with bailing wire when he was a young boy, when he was maybe 10 or 12 years old was retold that night, in the same way that I had remembered hearing it before on different occasions that were not that night. That is, I'd heard this story a lot and it was always pretty much the same.

But I still don't remember the exact reason why he earned this particular beating in the series of beatings that my father had received as a child. It might have had something to do with wearing shoes or not wearing shoes or having the wrong kind of shoes. The part about the shoes is still fuzzy to me, but I'm certain that my father had never been beaten with bailing wire before this time when he was 10 or 12 years old.

I also can't remember if my father knew why this beating was different and if that reason was in the retelling of the story every time he retold it but one other thing that was *always* different about this beating in the series of beatings my father received as a child was not only this use of bailing wire but also that after this particular beating my father ran away from home and never went back to school or the home where he had lived with his father. This is the same in every retelling of the story.

My father didn't tell this story differently than what I had remembered before this night, never made any hauling up gestures in its retelling, only maybe being more or less descriptive about bailing wire—about the existence of bailing wire and what it was used for—his gesture towards its existence and his memory of it being there. Of it, that is the bailing wire, not his father, or the leaving his home at age 10 or 12, being the center of the story.

One thing the False Memory Syndrome Foundation was particularly good at from the very beginning was changing the ways that sexual abuse stories were portrayed in popular media.

A study showed that in 1991, prior to the False Memory Syndrome Foundation's inception, of the stories about abuse in several popular press outlets "more than 80 percent of the coverage was weighted toward stories of survivors, with recovered memory taken for granted and questionable therapy virtually ignored."

However, three years later, and with the False Memory Syndrome Foundation's influence, "more than 80 percent of the coverage focused on *false* accusations, often involving supposedly false memory."

As you might remember, up to this point all the memories my father is sharing on that night are with my boyfriend. He is not talking to me, although I am sitting at the same small table right next to my boyfriend. He is only telling certain stories that end in a specific gesture. He does not tell the story of how he almost went to prison later in life. He is also not talking to my mother, who was, I think, sitting directly across from me at the table.

The workers have no choice but to tranquilize the man, much like the angry caged animal he has suddenly become, and he falls unconscious for a brief period, after which he appears to wake up slightly disoriented. He wakes up in the same chair where he initially submitted himself for memory implantation with, I think, all the same workers trying to hold him down.

Although the daughter had meant to keep this confrontation with her father private, because of her mother's actions she is forced to make a public statement. In her address she recounts a pattern of boundary and privacy violations by her parents, a pattern of inappropriate and unwanted sexualization by her father, a history of denial by her mother. She further articulates a pattern of intimidation and manipulation by both her parents since the inception of the Foundation that they now run.

I can't remember what my mother is doing at this dinner. I know that she has a seat at the table, but I think for the most part she and I were just silently witnessing my father haul himself through his memories for my boyfriend. This part of the memory doesn't feel unusual. I mean we were used to sitting silently. I don't remember if she had said anything up to this point in the conversation. I don't remember if my boyfriend has said anything up to this point in the conversation. I'm not sure that I've really said anything either. No one has contradicted my father's retelling of hauling himself up.

The thing that gets hard to track is that maybe he really is a secret agent. It's pretty unclear if we're now on a journey in his implanted vacation or his real life. This becomes the focus of the tension in the film. That is, I think we're meant to enter a kind of destabilized subjectivity.

According to fairly recent research, more than one out of four women have been raped. Statistics for incest are similar. We've all read this research, which may or may not be accurate when you think about how things get reported.

The False Memory Syndrome Foundation website doesn't seem to contradict this information about the prevalence of sexual violence against women, but other than this lack of contradiction, they do not address this issue at all. The issue they are most concerned with is how to verify real events that lead to memory and also how memories can't be verified.

I think I remember correctly that at what felt like mid-way through the bailing wire memory, my father turned to me rather abruptly and asked me a question directly. I don't remember what, if anything, he had said directly to me up to this point. But partway through the bailing wire story my father turned to me and pointedly said "I bet you don't even remember being spanked as a kid, do you?"

This question put to me so forcefully was already a presumption of a negation of something that might have existed but was forgotten.

I don't really remember what gesture I was trying to make by not having said anything up to this point. Maybe I was making the gesture of someone trapped into a kind of unwilling submission and now I was forced to recalibrate to the tension of being so suddenly addressed while having to agree that I didn't know something that maybe had happened. To conspire with something that wasn't.

The man finally leaves the office and, much like a real secret agent, skillfully and pretty violently avoids capture from a variety of familiar and unfamiliar characters attempting to detain him.

The Foundation asserts that False Memory Syndrome is especially destructive because the person who has confronted their parent of abuse assiduously avoids any evidence that might challenge the memory, making it resistant to correction. Also that the person, the adult child, may become so focused on the false memory that he or she may be effectively distracted from coping with the real problems in his or her life.

I suppose I should point out that up until this moment in the story at the dinner table I don't think my father had ever asked me anything about what I remembered from my own childhood. Not that I can recall anyway.

That is, my father would sometimes remember things for me but I don't think he ever asked me to agree or disagree with his account.

He would sometimes remember for me that he would call me a french whore when I wore a certain bathing suit when I was around maybe five years old. Or he would remember that he and I used to be such good friends until I was about three or four, sometimes comparing the current version of me negatively against the better version of me from before I was four years old.

He would regularly remind me of how for a long time that I couldn't say the letter "l" in "lollipop."

The thing is, he might actually be on Mars. Or maybe he's still in the chair back at the memory implantation office. It's a little unclear is what I'm trying to say. That's the whole underlying tension of the film. This uncertainty of where we are in this subjectivity.

I think it's probably accurate to say that I paused—that there was this pause of silence in the conversation where no one else, not my father or mother or boyfriend, was talking. I think that's right. I think I remember weighing the options of agreeing to my father's version of not remembering. Pros and cons.

I remember I felt a sense of gratitude that the thing that my father was asking me not to remember was not something that I felt any particular uncertainty or anxiety about. Because although I *did* remember what he was asking me to confirm I *did not* remember, it was not something that I felt I had to haul myself up from remembering.

I mean the movie *Total Recall* is essentially an action film. There are numerous car and foot chases, explosions, sex, gunplay. It's basically an action adventure film that is either a memory or not a memory of an action adventure film.

Like I might have already said, False Memory Syndrome is defined as a psychological condition in which a person remembers events that have not actually occurred, especially of childhood abuse, that are disputed by family members, and are often traumatic.

I didn't know this definition at the dinner table. I didn't know that the term "false memory" was a thing to be defined. I mean I guess it sounded pretty linguistically vague until I realized it wasn't.

Because the thing that I was asked to not remember was a thing of brutality but a thing that did not make me feel anxious or ashamed, I remember feeling slightly disappointed that the stakes felt so low for me to contradict my father. He did not ask me to not remember things for which I would have been more conflicted to not remember.

For example, he did not ask me to confirm that I did not remember the time he stabbed me with a fork all the way through my left hand while we sat at the dinner table, the other slightly larger table that we had when I was a child. I wasn't being asked to not remember how we didn't go to the hospital afterward, but I had difficulty writing comfortably, being left-handed, and it was hard to do schoolwork and homework for a while.

He did not ask me to not remember when he picked me up early from a recreational swim and there was a loaded gun on the front seat of the car or how he said that only I could talk him out of using it on himself as he drove me around while questioning my sincerity about how I wanted to talk him out of it.

He did not ask me to not remember the time he almost went to prison later in life or that one time time when I walked in to wake him up from a nap but he wasn't sleeping.

That is, he did not ask me to not remember a pattern of intimidation and manipulation that spanned across times when we both did and didn't have a family dog.

It felt almost too easy to contradict him. To make something in the place of where there was meant to be nothing.

I tried to ascertain the solidity of the memory of something I was meant not to know. But was something I knew.

Because I knew the whoosh of his belt slithering the loops and the thwack of the slap against the chair. I knew the buzzing sting on my bare skin accompanied by counting, and that I was never totally sure if it was counting up or counting down, whether it was increasing or decreasing and to what end. I knew how to try to telegraph by the level of squirm how much or how little punishment meant to my body and I knew how important it was to indicate or exacerbate it was making the proper impact. I knew the press of his thighs upon which I balanced. That awkward fumbling release.

And so I replied: Actually, I remember very clearly being spanked.

You have false memories, he said.

My mother corroborated his account, providing the expert testimony.

SPELL FOR FORGETTING

named in a small piece

circled and waning

      it's a casual anointment

like the desire to shift

almost imperceptibly

while folding

yourself

from
      and away

where this spell

is about you

INSTRUCTIONS

to look at the artifacts

but not believe they are
real,

and not know what you mean

by that

to hold these two things

side by side

the nothing/everything of it

slide the totality of this defect

back and forth along the

rougher stones discarded

in the pocket of a jacket

you always forget

pinches at the shoulders

before you

readjust

and try to make it seem

like it fits

SPELL FOR FORGETTING

visualize

a kind of

forgetfulness

                                              black ink

                                              white paper

                        maybe something red

                candled and centered

a circle

to be forgotten

made with chalk or spit

like something scratched in the dirt

but the person

                  or rather the paper

burned away

into an approximation of omission

still repeating

the words

with their meanings sloughed

leaving only the fact

and the want

INSTRUCTIONS

look at the walls

here

in this house

where you were built

and not remember them

hold out your tongue

and trace along the tendons

of what comes next
where the

allotments align and

click into certainty

then look again

when you can bear it

to
prove

that you can bear

it

SPELL FOR FORGETTING

affected:

just light out the erasure

and make your own

purified place

flush the fact and

form the names

do all of this

swallow the heat

of this forgetfulness

forming a crescent

jammed

in the roster

of the roost

of what wants to be forgotten

mouth the sinews

with the back of all you've got left

sound by sound

from beginning to end

until it feels like you're finished

and then recite it again

INSTRUCTIONS

make pilgrimages

to what the body can't   not

ever contain

parts of speech

parts of parts

grazing   the gap in this way

count the steps as you make them

the shape of the echo
your whisper makes inside your head
will be enough
for now
to seem a little upright

to re-ravel this contour

over and over
unfrayed and

then

also
to not

INSTRUCTIONS

hunkered and smothered

use the motion of grinding

to ignore the cramp
of making yourself

                          smaller

                            let your hands turn
                                     to dust
                                 in your hands

                               and never fail
to meet the eye of every stranger
making sure they see: *I'm fine it's fine*

                       everything is just fine

SPELL FOR FORGETTING

scourge the name

lettered on the

inside of a wound you

can't place the

provenance of

rake the scars on your

teeth

every day

until you metabolize all the fissures

        this form of a

        deserted open space

                in the shape of what

                you let them call you

INSTRUCTIONS

avoid mirrors and

windows

skip over pictures in the albums

bury in a practiced negligence

let your whole self be remade

in a rendering you let

happen without you

like one of those holes you've
read about

the kind with a   slow leak

smattering into

the simulation of extremities

now bury that too
just a little

there there
that's it

SPELL FOR FORGETTING

just imagine

cutting

all the little ties

all the little strings

just

imagine

every incident

every smell

every

time

INSTRUCTIONS

quelling
this body

like an especially privileged

kind of evidence

governing the

admissibility of

the forged and implicit

let the little details
stay cropped
wafting in the wreckage

of the tamed
and the stupidly buoyant

go on

cling to what's afloat

don't slip

SPELL FOR FORGETTING

realize the drag
inside the trigger

        irregular and reflective

                snagging on

hitching the
switch

        that is

        an opening of

        any sort at all

        for entry

        or exit

        shows up

        again and again

        whether you

        want it to

        or if you want

        really anything

        at all

go back

to fingering at the

blank   spot nagged

do it again

stop

do it again

SPELL FOR FORGETTING

eye of raptor

scent of hound

look for the markers

of acumen

            all of those things

            intractable and gleaned

            from the predatory

check the pulse

of the chased

and the chastened

fasten a kind of impossibility

in the rendering

of fat and fact

make what

was once

human

and

reform

what gets left

                  is it you

INSTRUCTIONS

               stumbled
        by the preponderance
            of something as
           stupid and elegant
          as honeysuckle juice
        that you always forget
      until it's greeted by the
     back of your own throat

eradicate the threat of what

        already exists

     what's agreed to

        in the end

   make the hollow of
                 the

          gullet

     a collusion

how is it that
you keep forgetting
that the stamen waits
as eagerly as you do
to be juiced

SPELL FOR FORGETTING

why not

represent your wrong doings

with stones or marbles and

a dark belief

meant for small mistakes

you can conceive

the only way

in

is through the

only-what-you-deserve

innocence brought upon

the need to gather it all

in the circumference of one cupped palm

just

place the infinite

under the soft part

of your

softest part

and breeze out the silence

of saying nothing

and feeling less

SPELL FOR FORGETTING

secluded thing :

just try and remember

        you'll want to

        draw an "X"

fill up the space

with the little things

discarded

and then

tamp down

resisting the urge to

lift up or

flatten against

whatever's there

for reckoning

once it's cast behind

close your eyes
start
walking

SPELL FOR FORGETTING

slip out

of what's

within the possible

and then

compress

back in

the sensation of

not being able

to simply

tidy up the entrails

the welts of ascent

     savor the hiss

     of consequence

     allowing it to steep

     in the biggest aperture you can find

INSTRUCTIONS

arriving with the ability

to be penetrated

the unrelented body

already a form of

consent

finger this certainty

with gentleness

like something you can count on

pressing as hard as you can stand into it and then
measure your
price

along the length of what you were

before you can even remember

Artifacts

You can see that their torsos are both exposed and their eyes are closed. The subject reports that only when she fell into the concavity of her father's body would she feel like she was doing something right. Breath for breath she matched him. She echoed him on the quick violent ascent with the long long too long pause at the top. Dizzy and urgent she waited to be released one foot dragging down the other, the mechanical movements of her body now switched off automatic. The subject wishing that the father both notice and not notice how hard she was trying to meet him in the middle. Then finally exhaling together, he one hitch ahead of her for driving this motion, sliding down this shared abyss and waiting to be filled up again. Eyes squinched. Chest tight. When asked all the subject can remember thinking is: *we are in this together, we are in this together, we are in this together.*

I mean, I can't show you where I
have n e u r o p l a s t i c thinning
of my cortical fields or anything.
so you're just going to have to take
my word for it that I would wake up
underneath this one particular chair
in my parent's bedroom having no
memory of having traveled from
one part of the house to the other
from that bedroom to the other and
that smell, the smell of the space
between the chair and the carpet I
guess I just want to say I get that this
isn't the full picture.

The only remaining photograph is of when the bunk beds were separated and the viewer is unable to visualize the second layer that would rest above the one featured, with a calico patchwork patterned blanket that the subject can not remember the feel of against her skin. The subject states she can't remember a time before the first time she remembers only that in that memory that is the memory of the first time she remembers in the memory the subject remembers knowing this was not the first time a series of befores this memory placed in the absence of what comes before it shaping the memory of what comes after it the subject states the memory is more of how she knew what she was supposed to do how the subject knew the role to play the subject remembers knowing the lines and the blocking remembering knowing without remembering a series of befores remembering playing her part and staging the scene for reproduction.

If you want to know
the truth I get that
you might want a
clearer sense of
what's going on
here like how I just
kind of frantically
searched my email
just now to look for
the exact phrase
my friend once said
to me which was
something like "this
sounds like a
trauma story but it's
so vague and I just
wish people would
just say what e x a
c t l y h a p p e n e
d
instead of hinting at
it" but I can't find
that email and I
can't
remember what my
friend said and
m a y b e I ' m
remembering it
wrong but that
might have to do
with the overactivity
in my amygdala that
makes it difficult t
o d e t e r m i n e
whether a
s t i m u l u s i s
threatening or not

The subject reports remembering seemingly random details that she still can't understand the significance of leading to gaps in the overall narrative. For instance, that clown painting that hung in the back bedroom at her grandfather's house for which there is no photograph but for the familiar feeling of this kind of honing in on something minor so basic and common. Or maybe it was a painting of a circus. Maybe just shapes. Subject reports uncertainty which disturbs the clarity of the overall narrative. As maybe there weren't clowns in the actual painting. It's possible that there were only clowns inserted later when the subject learned about the common fear of clowns and she wanted to normalize with other people's sense of collective fear.

It might help to say
that probably in
key regions in and
a r o u n d   t h e
hippocampus of my
brain you can tell
that if I'm about to
go to sleep and the
sound of a scratchy
radio comes on,
especially if it's just
the muffled sound of
people talking, or
a l s o j a z z   o r
something, I start to
feel panicked, can't
focus on anything
else and   how
quickly I have to
turn it, the radio,
off   and if that
shows up as a 6%
reduction in the
volume in two parts
of my hippocampus
then maybe you can
understand where
I'm coming from.

Managing to conjure neither a small or complete picture forming of a picture of a body in a two piece swimsuit caught in mid-movement across what appears to be a living room floor. Neither a small nor a complete body. Being barely able to stand to look at the flesh obscuring the bones. The open thighs. The partially exposed mouth. The not small but not complete picture actually conjured from a photograph and and not from inside the subject's actual memory. This picture conjured from the repeated retelling of this moment from the memories of others. How this image pauses at the body's own lack of grace through its unrepentant yet still invisible desirability. Still: no actual memory of this moment exists. The memory being smudged from the who held the camera.

I'd probably say
e v e r y t h i n g   if
everything I'd have to say can be
seen as the trajectory to more
severe
comorbid   psychopathology
and   compromised cognitive
psychosocial
functioning like when I had to
show that uncle my room and
stand   there unable   to   move
while he asked me about whether
I liked it and then answered for
me in the affirmative.

In a time before memory or a time without memory coming from inside the subject, that is, not having a memory to place this specific image in which the subject stands alone in a motel parking lot surrounded by black at what appears to be quite a distance from the photographer no other people in the frame. Little subject surrounded by nothing and still standing squarely and directly for the viewer. This performance of standing squarely and directly for the viewer, that is: standing there *really* looking at you, a memory that feels both familiar and unfamiliar to the subject as the various ways in which the subject remembers holding the body feel both familiar and unfamiliar.

If you want to know the
truth I realize that   the
way I'm telling this story
probably isn't making   a
lot of sense like I'm in a
kind of counterproductive
feedback loop sort of like
sort of like when very high
levels of stress hormones
can lead to cell death in
the very regions that are
supposed to tell the
system to stop production
I'm kind
of like rehearsing the
scene where my mother
casually tells me years
later that she always
thought there was
something between me
and my uncle and I mean
in this analogy of course
I'm the very region.

Here is another view in a smock dress patterned with the cartoon characters from *Winnie The Pooh*, a big red bow at the throat. Long flat hair. Yellow tights. The kind of smile one can't quite remember how to make. The assumption this was the picture taken on the first day of school with both the body featured as either a five or a six year old and one of a series of photographs wherein the subjects in the pictures were all wearing the same outfits—some with the father present and some with the mother and some with the older brother and some with each individual separately. Subject admits to not having a memory of this specific day of these specific groupings but a series of memories in uncovering these photographs throughout her lifetime. Subject strains to recall the feelings that seems to be presented in the photograph as a rehearsal in how to move the body in relation to the space around it.

It's not that I am
trying to be vague I
really do want to try
to tell y o u
everything or at least I
think I want to tell you a
clearer narrative of how
I got a headache every
single day that one week
in first grade but I might
have delays in, I mean I
might have deficits of, I
mean I
might have failures of
m u l t i - s y s t e m
a c h i e v e m e n t s   i n
motor, emotional,
b e h a v i o r a l ,
l a n g u a g e ,
psychosocial, social,
and cognitive skills,
that is at least I know
that I asked to go to
the nurse's office
every day that week
but I'm not entirely
sure that my head
hurt.

Center of the frame surrounded by what are maybe toys or clothes or other household items it's not immediately easy to tell the how the body is situated in a time before memory not having anything to cling to from this apartment before the apartment more clearly remembered. Just a squat blotch of a child she once was in this frame of textured carpet and misplaced objects she is staring directly into the camera looking back at an angle to suggest surprise perhaps or maybe something else it is impossible to chart the emotion in her face or what might have been the conditions under which this moment was captured or by who. The subject recalls only one memory from this apartment before the apartment she remembers just one memory of being carried half sleeping from her parents' car—carried by her father her entire body fitting in the uppermost part of his as they traveled chest to chest and she remembers looking to the top of the stairs that led to their apartment and very clearly seeing what could only in her mind be described a monster and mumbling to her father about its presence and hearing him say that monsters weren't real.

SPELL FOR REMEMBERING

cower and crouch

bend and bow

set

the something

you've forgot

its setting

fixed from

all of

what was

and the charm

of the gleaned

leave it

in its place

where you leave it

find this one lost thing

and hold it

tight in the cleft of your favored palm

                    just like that

CHARMS

you take the little hints
at how to navigate

leaving the high notes for
everyone else

trace the lament
threaded in
even the smallest
of things

the cantering incandescence

tight, *tighter*

like that resistance
toward naming anything
with its given name

unopened and still

the wish
you don't ask
someone to make
for you
turning to razors
in the tomorrows
of your tongue

SPELL FOR REMEMBERING

make sure you believe in it

ready your head

till the lines

remember each path

do all this again

do it one more time

CHARMS

hobbled by
each and every
futurity
not owned

you try to slither away
away from the confines
of the
superseded and tucked
but
your snails are all salted
participles parcelled

SPELL FOR REMEMBERING

lie down beside yourself

in a white room

with two doors

open or closed

and chant the following

list of ways

you are both more

and less than

the sum of

your parts

a product

still negligible

somehow

        now

        the person

        you've imagined

        is it

            you

CHARMS

run
the tip of your finger
over the concavity
of an index
of
every instance where
you write *mouth*
when you mean to say
smother
this metronome
of scarcity
ticking away
the ambivalence
of what to
want
and
it's hard to know what to

carry forward

time folding in on itself

like it does

enormous and clumsy

muzzled
and spent

SPELL FOR REMEMBERING

gather materials and

situate what's missing

light the candle

     open your bottle

     place your desire into

     that space

     while holding it

look

until you feel

something and

then wait

until it's

 something else

CHARMS

ignore
the cast off pennies

leave
the feet intact
on rabbits

mow all
the clovers

a substitute
for a corpse
you call your own
tempts a gesture
almost extant
enough
to pass

flip the horseshoe
shoo the
crickets keep your
coins in your
pockets
at the well

SPELL FOR REMEMBERING

cast a circle or

sit facing south

take what's just out of

your grip

sprinkle it with salt

keep it in between the teeth

pebbled rough and tangible

tell it everything until it's

glowing with

something else

you forgot

CHARMS

and even though
you know
it is impossible
(maybe)
to find yourself
in this rendering

made
remade
made again

go ahead and scratch
at the smudged
and blundered

the things
abandoned
and forged
in a blur
the moment
they happen

a smear or blot
that renders   is rendered

seen   unseen
known   and
otherwise tucked

neglecting the ways you are
frayed
marking the
invisible ways
you betray
what you're
not sure
you remember
or not
what you are
or not

the marks
the marks
the marks

unmaking

SPELL FOR REMEMBERING

in a holder

that is easy to carry

walk from room to room

making the motions of

nothing muscled

careful now: don't fall

CHARMS

take
absence
as a form of
absolution

parts contained
insoluble
and sledged

sieved
to a
pit

chalk the chasm
breath for breath
then

marshed
and burned

consecrate
the
remnants
carry them around
in your
hidden heart

the heft
a weight to
redistribute
to trick the scales

SPELL FOR REMEMBERING

in a manner similar to the kind of

shutting up you're comfortable with

instead of finding purchase

the past is dragging you down

so take some time to consider the

methods of free fall

start with an opening of any sort

in the center

keeping it closed

seeing whatever

flutters

in that certain spot

of sunlight

CHARMS

husk

the expectation

of how to hold yourself

in a chair

or other object

assumption of limbs

unlimned

cockling to cancel out

what to contain and where

and someone

keeps sending

the birds in

to carry the trailcrumbs

away

beakful to beak

swallow to swallow

unnested

trying to think
of another word for
thresh

SPELL FOR REMEMBERING

close your eyes at the very end

and it's almost like a flashback

The Question

The thing is we weren't really friends anymore by this point. I mean, it's probably not relevant to the story or maybe it is, but pretty much by this point I don't think we were friends anymore. We had gone to elementary school together, but maybe only fifth and sixth grades and we'd hung around in the same loose group of maybe six friends at the time. I don't really remember if I'd ever hung out with just her, but it's possible. She was kind of electric in a way that made you want her to like you. That is, I think she already knew how to shoplift by the time we'd met and she was definitely the first person to play that new GoGos album at a sleepover. It felt like a gift to get invited is what I'm trying to say.

Parents weren't really part of the overall narrative from what I recall. Rather: each other's parents. I knew she lived alone with her mother in an apartment and her dad lived somewhere a little north in the hills by the beach. I'm sure I'd spoken to her mother but I can't conjure a specific conversation or even really more than the basic sketches of her mother's face. I think if I'm honest her mother seemed kind of maybe not hinged together but only because she wasn't entirely tucking herself in in the way I was used to. She tucked herself in differently. I can only just barely remember her. Her mother, I mean. Though, to be fair, this story isn't really about her mother.

Anyway, all of the maybe six of us were fairly good friends in elementary school. I mean in fifth and sixth grade. We probably slept over at each other's houses all the time, shoplifted makeup that we only sometimes wore, stole candy and sometimes clothes, listened to the GoGos and tried to look like them. I can't remember one single specific conversation that we had or really anything but the most basic impressions about each of these six friends, but I'm pretty certain that we spent almost every day together at least until we split apart for junior high. Now that I think about it maybe there were only four of us.

I'm trying to figure out a way to tell this story so I'll just say that the junior high school ran seventh, eighth and ninth. There were a few kids from elementary school, kids that I had grown up with since kindergarten, and some of those kids followed me to junior high. But I don't think any of the six or four of us initially. That is, the junior high set up was like most public schools in that there were a lot of small elementary schools that fed into one large middle school. The public elementary school that I had gone to split its students into two different middle schools: one in a wealthy neighborhood, one in a more working class neighborhood. I went to the working class school.

So, as you'd expect, in seventh grade I made a whole new set of friends, and pretty much stopped hanging out with the kids I'd known since kindergarten. I guess you would say that I was kind of popular, but I wouldn't have said that about myself at the time. I didn't have a lot of attachment to things or maybe even people at the time. There's a lot of this story that I'm not really saying but only because I'm not really sure how relevant everything is. My new friends also liked the GoGos. Shoplifted sometimes.

She turned up at my school in eighth grade. Maybe it was ninth grade. She turned up after I was, I guess, pretty popular maybe. A friend recently said to me that if I wasn't sure if I was popular in junior high then I probably was, so I probably was pretty popular. I hadn't kept in touch with her since elementary school. At least I don't think so. But of course we still kind of knew each other. I can't remember if we'd even seen each other once in between sixth and eighth or maybe ninth grade. I don't think so, but we might have. I can't remember anyway. Maybe this is important or maybe it's not.

She was pretty popular in fifth and sixth grade I guess. That electricity thing. I think maybe at the time I understood popularity as being someone that multiple boys wanted to kiss. She was this kind of popular in elementary school but maybe she wasn't this kind of popular anymore. I don't think I was ever that kind of popular, but that might be a thing that's hard to track. At least I don't think I was ever this kind of popular. I mean I had friends. It's kind of hard to remember. Anyway, this part doesn't really matter.

The junior high was small enough that people noticed that she was new to the eighth grade. Maybe it was ninth grade, I'm not really sure. People noticed her, but in a way that wasn't entirely electric. I don't know if this is the right way to tell this story, but I did kind of start to feel a pressure from her to be friends again, a pressure that I didn't want. That is, I think she was trying to be friends with me again or she wanted to leverage that old friendship into something useful to her now in either the eighth or ninth grade. But we weren't really friends anymore. I might have this all wrong. I feel like I'm telling this story all wrong.

I'm trying to say that I don't know that we were really friends at this point. She had made some moves to try to get noticed even more and some of my new friends asked me to vouch for these moves. I'm pretty sure I remember not vouching for her. I wasn't a good friend to her in this situation, so maybe now I'm telling the story that we weren't really friends. It may or may not be relevant that at some point I participate in writing a fake advice column for the school newspaper which is kind of mocking these moves she was trying to make at the time. I think it was Exhibit O. Or maybe Exhibit D. It may or may not become relevant later. I'm not sure where we are in the timeline.

I'm not entirely clear how this happens but she winds up spending the night at my house pretty soon after arriving at my school in eighth or ninth grade. I think it was probably still fall—still early in the school year that is—and after a high school football game held at the community college across the street from our junior high. These were the kind of games that I'd regularly gone to with my new set of friends, though I've never been much of a football fan. I'm not sure but this might have been the last high school football game I attended, but there's no real way to verify that. Anyway I think at some point the defense attorney pulls the records of the school calendar. I'm not sure if the advice column is written at this point. I do feel fairly sure that we're not really friends, but here's the part that makes me feel a little uncertain about that: after hanging out with a group of my new friends at the game that night, she invites herself to spend the night at my house and I relent. It's possible that I felt a little ashamed of the not vouching for her. It's possible that I thought that maybe we actually were friends. I might have just been unable to say no.

I don't really know how we got to my house or what we did there until we fell asleep. There was kind of a big effort later on to get the records for what was on television that night, but I don't have access to those records only a reference to Exhibit B.

Anyway at least I remember saying yes or being unable to say no and that I fell asleep before she did. I mean I always fell asleep first in these kinds of situations and I don't have any memory of being awake while she was asleep, so I'm pretty certain that I fell asleep first. I remember being in the living room: me on the couch, her on the reclining chair that was directly across from the very small dining room table in the apartment where I grew up. I'm sure that we watched television, probably a series of music videos that ran on a loop at the time. Maybe even something by the GoGos. And then I fell asleep. You could probably look up the records of what was on TV that night to get more of a full picture. I mean somebody eventually did this.

I do remember pretty clearly that I woke up in the middle of the night and I noticed that she wasn't in the chair where I had last seen her. Feeling that kind of familiar disoriented shame that I once again had fallen asleep first, I remember going to look for her. I went to my room at the back of the apartment to see if she had moved to my bed but she wasn't there either. I can't remember if the TV was on or off but I noticed that the front door was open. I'm kind of making up the events here as they seem logical to me now. Apparently at some point I made some kind of diagram, Exhibit Q maybe. I went outside and found her crying on the steps just outside the door to our apartment. That is, the steps right outside that led to the upstairs units.

Most people already have a pretty idealized idea of the town where I grew up. I guess in their minds it's only a glamorous place full of bounty. But the place that I remember growing up in was more sharp edges and kind of low-grade industrial filth than anything. I was always kind of embarrassed to have friends over and some of that is about the apartment building where I lived.

I mean, it was a Hollywood kind of town. A lot of TV shows and movies of the era featured the same streets that my new friends from junior high and I wandered around endlessly until we went back to someone's house to watch those streets show up on TV. We'd wander around half or even entirely drunk from Boone's Farm that we would get older men to buy us from the liquor store and mostly forget about the characters we'd watch later do the same thing more elegantly and with a sound blurring laugh track. So it's easy sometimes to switch the narratives a little and forget which town I grew up in: the one I remember or the one on TV.

Like I tried to say, we probably weren't friends at this point, but in this story I'm going to try to replicate the feeling of a kind of concerned worry for her in this moment where she is outside on the steps leading to the upstairs units of the apartment building. I'm pretty sure that I've got that right. I don't remember feeling anything but worry. But that's kind of a hard thing to access. I'm not sure I'd ever had a friend or maybe not totally a friend (whichever it was she was at this point) do something like sit outside on the steps and cry in the middle of the night before. So it seems pretty reasonable that I'd be worried about her.

I mean, yes, there was this beautiful beach that buttressed the entire west side of the town I grew up in. You've definitely seen it in hundreds of movies. But there was also the tar that stuck to our feet, the black stains it would leave. We were constantly coming up with new remedies to combat it. Like was direct scraping better or soaking with baby oil first. It wasn't until much later that I figured out that tar wasn't just naturally occurring on beaches. At the time, I thought that was just how beaches worked.

I don't exactly remember what she told me. I don't exactly remember if I believed what she told me, but I remember that I didn't *not* believe it either. I was asked about the specificity of what I did and didn't remember in this moment over and over and I still don't exactly know what she did or didn't say.

Maybe to tell this story I could say that my parents both were and weren't part of the overall narrative at that point. I probably already said that. I'm not exactly sure where we are in the timeline but I was probably both overly aware and also not aware at all of my parents by seventh, eighth or maybe ninth grade. This seemed pretty much the same across the families of all my friends, though it wasn't something we ever talked about. I didn't really know it at the time, but a lot of my friend's families lived in Section 8 housing, or were on some kind of public assistance, or otherwise probably in some kind of economic terror all the time, even while the streets around us were on TV. There was a kind of colluded disengagement around this. We all tacitly agreed to not let on that we were all in on the inside joke.

I'm trying to say that a lot of us, whatever grade we were in, were left on our own all the time. We used this indifference to what at the time felt like our advantage, spending endless hours just walking around, either half or totally drunk, smoking shake we stole out of our parents or older siblings dressers, sucking the smoke out of reconfigured apples or bent up Pepsi cans. It's easy to see from this vantage that we were corroborating a kind of reaction to the world where our parents weren't there to watch us. Maybe performing a kind of unknown third thing that wasn't childhood or adulthood in that whatever place of our own making. I mean it was not uncommon to feel like an adult walking around on the streets where all sorts men would expose themselves to you, make kissing noises as they passed. Where men would routinely follow you home, pleading for your attention. Buy you cheap fizzy wine in hopes you'd ride with them in their cars so they could snake their calloused hands between you and your clothes. That is, in this casual neglect, some of us understood early on how the relentlessness of male attention could get you a pretty cost-effective high.

Maybe I should try to tell this story by just talking about my father. I'm pretty sure I had both no interest and a lot of interest in my father by this point. But that might have come later. No, that's probably accurate. I will say that I knew at this point he was always the most electrified thing in any room. Maybe that's what I'm trying to gesture towards. That I was never not aware of him, whether he was there or not. That he had a way of making people feel really chosen if he wanted to. That he could make me feel really chosen. When he wanted to. That that choice, or even I guess the absence of that choice, could feel kind of electric.

If I'm already going to pull back a little bit it feels impossible to tell this story without telling the story of my father and my father's father and probably even the father before that. I mean, of course this is a story of my father but all those other fathers are in there and this story isn't possible without them. I guess I want to tell you that after their mother died, my father's three sisters moved out of their father's house, each before they turned fourteen years old, about the age that you're usually in ninth grade. I only later learned that this was to get away from my father's father. Maybe even my father himself and his two brothers, one younger and one older than my father, maybe they too left for this reason. They all left their father's house to get away from their father before they would have finished junior high is what I'm trying to say.

I guess then I want to tell you that I remember feeling gratitude when my father's father died, which was around this time, around when I was in eighth or ninth grade. That's probably not the full story. I did feel grateful although there are probably other things I felt. Other parts of the story. The story of his children all leaving him around the same age that I am in this story wasn't probably something I had put together completely at that time. I'm pretty sure that I wasn't aware that I wasn't the first to kneel alongside my father's father and have him silently but insistently place himself in my hands. That that clubhouse he built specially in the backyard with only one entrance was a place I never wanted to be in alone wasn't the first sort of pen he had built. It was impossible to know that I wasn't the first.

I'm not sure that this is important to this story that I'm trying to tell but it is the story of my father's father but also of my father and the things I both knew and didn't know about him. And about how I thought that maybe I was the only one that knew them. I guess I'm trying to locate the ways I had learned not to be surprised by things by including this part about what I knew and didn't. I'm still not sure what to keep in and what to leave out.

I want to say that when I found her on the stairs, when she told me what I don't exactly remember, I don't remember feeling surprised to hear it. I think that's right. I don't remember feeling like what she was telling me was surprising. I remember feeling a kind of panicked shame that was probably more about the story of my father's father's father than anything else. But also to be sitting outside of the apartment that I was ashamed to bring people to and here we were sitting outside of it. The shape and density of that being familiar. Of being given something that held a longer and more complicated timeline than that present moment. I'm trying to tell you that being told to hold something like that, both slippery and inevitable, felt familiar almost as soon as she started talking.

I don't know if I should tell you this but there's also the part of this story where at some point around seventh or eighth but definitely ninth grade, my father and mother leave my older brother and me at home while they go on a series of long trips. By the time I was seven years old we had, my brother and I, been left at home unsupervised every day when my parents were at work, doing all the nightly tasks of dinner and homework and putting ourselves to bed without them to assist or cajole us. But during this part of the story they didn't come home for weeks at a time. I mean I think that was the general sense of things.

So wrapped inside this story there is the story of where my brother and I stay home and spend the insufficient amount cash that is left on the counter for us by our parents who leave for weeks at a time. We spend that money maybe on food but mostly on the kind of cheap beer that has a puzzle on the inside of the cap. We throw a series of endless parties, one merging into the next, heaving a trash can from the alley outside my bedroom window to the middle of our living room, maintaining a certain kind of order but accelerating the cockroach population.

We left the trashcan right next to the reclining chair in the living room and tried to collect all the beer bottles and cigarette butts as we went along. We spent a lot of time watching Michael Jackson's *Thriller* video, which was scheduled to play at certain points during the day on MTV. We also kept watching that movie *Creepshow* somehow always managing to start at the scene where the man is overrun by cockroaches, letting the art and reality of the moment smudge a little again, like it did on the streets.

I'm not exactly sure where this part fits in the timeline but there is definitely a span of time where instead of going to school or the grocery store to buy food, we watch *Thriller* and *Creepshow* over and over, drinking novelty beer and solving its puzzles while throwing a series of endless parties, with a trash can in the middle of our living room right next to the couch and the reclining chair. There's a part inside this part of the story where some friend of my brother's, 22 to my 14, advises me to keep my underwear on if I'm not planning on fucking someone, his cum on my leg becoming a knot I distract myself with worry over. When in defiance of gravity and the mechanics of procreation until I finally get my period, late and painful and mine, it gets intertwined in this narrative arc. I'm not sure why it feels important to tell you any of this. I'm not sure if I'm situating it right. The timeline is still so disorganized. Maybe I'm trying to make excuses for something that's still a little blurry. I don't really want to tell you the story of my brother, so I'm going to leave the rest of that part out.

It's maybe at this point when I feel like she and I are most like real friends. I should say I mean the part where we're sitting on the stairs leading up to the upper apartments. I feel like maybe at this point she now knows me better than anyone else. I'm probably adding that feeling in now, but it feels accurate. I know I didn't testify to this, but I want to include it. This connection to what didn't surprise me and how that forged this feeling of closeness.

I do want to tell you this one thing that is a very small story about my brother. I don't know exactly how old we are, but at some point my father, my brother and I go on a weekend trip to a nearby desert vacation spot without my mother. Maybe I'm in the fourth grade. I have braces and neck gear that I wear all day because I think it will make the overall time I have to wear it shorter somehow. I could be in fifth grade. I don't really know. There were two beds, side to side in the hotel room and my brother and I were sharing one of them, my father in the other. I was already asleep, having said goodnight to my father at the bar earlier, the bar at the hotel where we are staying, but when I wake up, the room is dark save the light from the bathroom, and I hear what I think is dripping water.

We made our way back to my room at the back of the apartment, coming inside from having been on the stairs outside. It would be easier if I could show you the diagram they entered into evidence. I don't remember where she slept, it's possible I just had a twin bed by this point, but I remember curling up on the floor, blocking the door to my room like a dog. Feeling the door press into my back, sharp and insistent as my father tried to open the door in the morning, angry that he couldn't get what he wanted.

It was not dripping water. It was something else that I only learn in this moment to identify. There was also my father's voice and what I think is my mother's but was quickly revealed not to be. I tried repeatedly to wake my brother who is lying next to me, both urgently and clandestinely, because I want him to hear this noise that is not water and to know this thing I now know alongside me. But he doesn't wake up and in the morning in the sunlight by the pool I'm not sure how I tell him about what happened while he was sleeping. But I am sure that he looks me straight in the face and tells me over and over again that whatever I am trying to tell him that happened the night before didn't happen. That what I thought happened wasn't real. I simply imagined the whole thing.

I don't think I testified to this fact, but I want to make sure you heard this part. This part where I was curled like a dog.

This story is probably also a little bit about my mother. I'm not really sure what I should say about my mother except that I guess you could say that the story of my mother is basically a series of stories where she is repeatedly electrified by my father. I'm not sure if there is a line going back to my mother's mother's mother of all the women that found a man who electrified them in this particular way. That is, it's probably not that hard to imagine. I guess I'm trying to say that most of my memories of my mother at this point are the stories in which she chooses my father and the stories in which she wants only to be chosen by him. If I'm honest, I'm not sure I could tell you many other stories about my mother. This might be the wrong way to tell the story of my mother, but this is also part of the story about my mother.

I don't remember much from after that morning where I'd blocked my bedroom door like a dog, after the stairs, the things I can't quite remember what she told me. I don't remember if we ate breakfast together or hung out later in the day, what, if anything, we said to my father. Whether she came back to school for the rest of eighth or maybe ninth grade. I'm not sure where the timeline is tracking at this point. I just want to say I know she doesn't continue going to junior high with me but I don't know when exactly that change happens.

There is this moment, though. In the car. After the police station. Before what happens next. Where my mother and I are in a kind of protected space. I still think about this moment a lot. It is so unlike all the other stories I can tell you about my mother. And while we're there in that space because of my father who put us there, this moment feels somehow outside of him. It feels like it's just about the two of us. I still remember how surprised even while it was happening that I was having this moment with her. I was so loosened by the day, I had no way to filter out what to say and somehow this was fine in this moment. To have her receive me. To be held in that space with just her. And just up until the moment where she ruined it, where she shifted the balance back where it had always been, it felt in that small spot of sunlight, almost electric.

I can't remember if I have to testify at the first and then the next trial to how I felt when she told me what I only kind of remember on the stairs. I'm not sure if my opinions ever came up in the arguments. I think I remember a lot of questions about what she specifically said to me, but not about whether or not what she said felt like a surprise. I don't actually know. By the time I thought to access the court transcripts, they were already destroyed.

Maybe it will be helpful in trying to tell this story to say that I think it's also around this time, between seventh and eighth grade, that my mother tries to kill herself. Or maybe that's not quite right. Maybe "helpful" is the wrong word but I still don't know which parts to leave out. Maybe the more accurate story is that my mother tries to be chosen by my father and the method is through a kind of gesture of trying to kill herself. This story is getting away from me a little. I'm trying to tell this story as best as I remember it.

Something I always forget to include in the story about my father is that well before the time I am born all the way up to the first trial, my father drinks, just like his father and maybe his father's father before that. Maybe it's before the second trial that he stops drinking. I'm not really sure. What I'm trying to say, but I always forget to say, is that pretty much every day until he went on trial, my father drank at least a fifth of gin, usually more than a fifth of gin depending on his schedule. I don't know why I always forget about this part. I don't even know if it's important. Both the fact of it and the forgetting of that fact. I don't even know if fifth is the right measurement. I think it is.

Maybe it won't help you to understand the story but the summer between seventh and eighth grade my father's mistress comes to stay with us for the summer and, although I never see or hear it, probably has sex with my father on the couch in the living room where I later wake up and find my friend has gone missing. Maybe "mistress" is the wrong word. I think my mother slept in my parents' bedroom that summer, which is more adjacent to the dining room, while my father's mistress and my father sleep in the living room with the dining room more in front of them than to the side. Then one night, she, that is my mother, maybe decides that it is time for my father to choose her again and so she tries to kill herself and then retreats to my bedroom at the back of the apartment. She lies down in my bed, streaked with blood and longing, when her attempt fails. This never comes up at trial and it might not be very relevant.

I'm pretty sure I remember a series of phone calls. Not too many. Maybe three phone calls over the course of a year and I think it's always her calling me. Rather, it seems impossible to me that I would have called her. It really might have been only one phone call. I don't really know. I think in these phone calls she said she felt like she had to tell her mother about what we talked about on the stairs and I think in these phone calls I begged her not to. I probably tried to appeal to her as a friend, using some of the same gestures that had helped me become kind of popular. I wish I didn't have to tell you this part, where I am begging her to say nothing, but it's definitely part of the story. I don't know if she testified to that fact or not. I'm pretty sure I didn't.

The truth is I only remember the smallest bit of what I was asked to remember and not remember, what I was asked to attest to or denounce at the two different trials. I remember almost nothing of when I was, according to the only documents I could access, the person who testified more than any other witness in either case before the court. I am listed as spending more time in questioning for both the defense and the prosecution. That is, there are a series of witnesses for both trials, some of which are the same and some of which are different, yet I am listed as testifying more times and for a longer duration than any other witness in either. It's probably around this time that I learn the term "star witness."

I don't really remember if the phone calls and what came after happened during the same year. That is, if it was eighth grade, or the next year. I'm pretty sure though that I was in ninth grade when I'm questioned by the police. I don't really remember what they asked me. But I think it's probably accurate that most of my answers to their questions were vague. There's some kind of point made at the first trial about the inconsistencies between what I said then when I was first questioned and what I said now on the stand.

I used to always say "star witness" when I've tried to tell this story, usually in a set of dismissive anecdotes that skirts around the details. "Oh I was the star witness for two separate trials once," I'll say when someone asks about if I've ever gone to court. But honestly I don't really know what "star witness" means except in relation to how it's used on TV. I think I used to think it meant that this story was only possible because of me.

I remember being hot and disoriented in the storage closet or (maybe it was a spare classroom I can't really remember) at my junior high school where the police questioned me. I mean, I knew that something was coming ever since I begged her not to tell her mother. But I didn't know exactly what was coming. How I kept thinking this was a room I'd never been in before. I still have those dreams where I find an extra room in my house I never noticed before. Maybe everyone has this dream sometimes. That kind of generalized fear again. I'm just trying to locate myself in that room where they're questioning me about what I remember.

It's possible that I always forget the part where my father drinks because there isn't much that changes after he stops drinking except that we use the cabinet to the left of the sink for something other than gin. I mean I can't really point to anything substantially different about my father once he finally quits drinking for the last time. I go with him to AA for a number of months at some point though I am never entirely sure why he brings me with him. I think maybe I was meant to witness his sacrifice. I can't think of any other reason.

I do kind of remember thinking in that moment that we had each picked a side: my brother and I. I mean I think I remember thinking that. I decided in that moment that the two sides were looking at things directly or participating in the game of looking away. And I could see that he wasn't going to look and I was. That's what it felt like anyway. That's what it meant to me: me looking and him not. It sounds kind of dramatic when I say it that way but I guess I hadn't noticed how much he never looked before that. How I thought we were both seeing the same thing and I didn't know until that moment by the pool that what we saw was different like those "explain the color blue" tests. I can't tell if this difference in blue is relevant to this story, the one I keep trying to tell, but I guess it's a little bit of a part of the story I'm trying to tell. I'm just trying to explain something that is sort of a story about my brother. I'm still going to leave the rest of it out.

It seems unlikely in that way that makes me think I'm fusing a few different narratives but I think that I'm remembering correctly that after I'm questioned about the conversation on the stairs, the police drive me to the station and on the way they stop to get me a vanilla milkshake at the Fosters Freeze that is near the junior high school, on the other side of the community college where the high school would usually play football. This part of the story always confuses me: why I had to go to the police station all the way across town with them after they'd questioned me in the hot forgotten room and why they bought me a milkshake. I don't think anyone ever asked me about these series of hours where I'm questioned, driven, fed.

On TV, the actors playing witnesses can talk for as long as they want, often adding details the actors playing attorney didn't ask for, and this can be used against them. If you've ever testified in court, you probably already know that every courtroom scene on TV is basically a lie. I mean if we're both going to look at this the same way. The way that testimony gets written on TV is a performative shallow echo of the idea of what it means to bear witness. Actor witnesses are always accidentally bragging about something that incriminates them. They always have a chance to fully explain something, sometimes in a way that trips them up, but never in a way that gives them less to say.

If you're not an actor pretending to testify in court you probably already know how the real thing feels like an endless series of stoppages. A caught in the throat kind of restraint. Where the answers can only be "yes" or "no" and you are never allowed to go back over anything you said, to contradict or amend what has been recorded. I mean, if you've been in that seat, which sits higher than some but lower than others, kind of sequestered off from the rest of the room, you already know what I'm talking about. It's hard not to feel like a caged animal. That sense of displacement and forced acquiescence. How it can press into you, if you know what I mean. It's pretty hard to forget.

It may or may not be relevant that even though I am only in ninth grade at this point I make my mother stop for cigarettes on the way home from the police station, where she has had to come pick me up after I am questioned and then transferred. Even though I have never smoked in front of my mother I make her stop to get me cigarettes, not flinching when she asks me my preferred brand. I remember her not only buying them for me but letting me smoke one after the other in her car, although in my memory I am in the driver's seat despite not yet being old enough to drive. I remember almost nothing of what we actually said to each other but it was a pretty singular moment. It was just the two of us in the car and I remember feeling not only kind of electrified by her attention but also ashamed to say how good it felt to be chosen in this moment. I probably shouldn't leave that part out.

The timeline is getting a little confused. I can tell you there are a series of things that I know happened after the phone call and the milkshake and the cigarettes. I think I forgot to say that at some point in this narrative my father had moved three states away from where this story has so far taken place and before my mother comes to get me from the police station I first hear the word "extradited." I definitely remember it making a linguistic impression.

It's probably obvious by now that in series of things that happen there are two criminal trials in which evidence is presented to decide if what I can't quite remember the specifics of, that was told to me on those stairs leading to the upstairs units of the apartment building, was true or not and why or not. I'm not sure if I've made it clear but I'm basically the main voice of the defense, that's the side my father is on, for the entirety of both trials, despite the fact that the trial's strategy changes completely from one event to the next. I am also inexorably the main voice of the prosecution. While this process takes up the length of most of my years in high school (the lead up to trial, the first trial, the hung jury, the second trial, the second hung jury), I remember very little of the specifics. No one in my family ever talked about these events in the years after they happen. Not once.

Although there is one time right before my father and I have a sort of fight years later, after which we intentionally stop talking to each other for about a year and a half, where he vaguely gestures towards having given something up or maybe having been betrayed I can't really remember what the exact phrasing was but something about having had to bear the burden of something I had done to him. For some reason I got the sense that he was maybe talking about this story of this time when I was in junior high and then high school but he wouldn't elaborate about this sacrifice, so it's possible he was talking about something else.

I've tried endlessly to reconstruct what those years held and the ways in which things overlap and I still can't make sense of them. Like there is the time somewhere after the police station but somehow before the extradition, where my father yells at me on the phone from three states away for being hit by a car, and I am pulled out of school to make a case for insurance. How afterwards I'm left to wander the streets somewhat regularly for the rest of ninth grade, and to stop being my particular kind of popular. At some point my father's mistress falls out of the picture, but that might be just natural attrition or it might have something to do with this story I have no idea. There is also how I have my first boyfriend at the same time that I'm testifying more than any other person at the second trial. The sloppy intense making out in the back seat of my first car somehow both in and outside of this timeline. There's how we must have had a school football team when I finally get to high school but I have no memory of ever attending another game. How I have to ask my friends who may or may not have still been my friends to testify in a series of trials defending my father. How some say yes.

That is only to say here is where it would make sense to reconstruct the narrative of those two trials, the evidence submitted, and all the exhibits, but I'm pretty sure I don't remember anything about them right. There is no one I can check to see if my story is right, each participant: my father, my mother, my friend who might not have been my friend who I never speak to again after that last phone call, aren't on record to corroborate my memory. Which is to say there are timelines that are lost to me and the transcripts were destroyed before I had a chance to look at them.

·

I'm pretty sure that at the time I felt my role in this story was to suspend the timeline of my father and my mother and my father's fathers and my mother's mothers and choose the moment, over and over or a series of years and two separate criminal trials where I am asked under oath, to remember things differently from how I remembered them. To choose this version of my father you could only see by not looking directly at him. I was meant to bear witness to this version of a life, despite the way the door jammed into my back, over everything else I may have known.

I'm trying to say that I'm pretty sure that my role was to be electrified about a specific narrative of what happened in that moment on the stairs leading up to the upper units of the apartment building and to remember this narrative with such conviction so as to avoid conviction. The threat that I might remember things incorrectly or choose the wrong narrative as testimony was electrified into me over and over again so that the sting on my skin would help me remember it. I think I performed this correctly but, like I said, I can't show you the transcripts.

If you've never heard the term "hung jury" I can tell you what I think it means: in the two trials that take many years to construct and execute, no one who is asked to do so ever comes to a unanimous decision about what did or didn't happen before I woke up to find my friend outside on the steps leading up to the upper units of the apartment building. That is, there's no official story of the narrative you're supposed to believe on record because of the two separate groups that were meant to pick out the truth, none could agree what it was or wasn't.

It's probably no surprise here that at some point much later in the timeline I haul myself to the downtown county courthouse to request the trial documents still available for reproduction. It's a gesture I try to make to verify that at least part of what I remember actually happened. When I get the slim file they have on record, all the names are there but it seems like the dates are all wrong.

There is one moment though. In the chair. I'm not sure if it's the first or second trial. It's probably the second. After hours of trying in stops and starts to reconstruct what I did and didn't remember, after having been sworn in again and again, after referring to exhibits and contradictory arguments, I was asked a very simple question. That is, I was asked a question that I don't think had been asked of me up until this point. A question for which I had no answer. Which I probably still don't. But I had gotten this far in the story, in the timeline, in the chair, in this exact moment and I remember looking over to my father who sat at the defendant's table, forced into silence by the rules of the court. Maybe a little too tranquilized by the scene to thrash around.

This question a request for a confirmation about something that maybe wasn't there. About my father, yes, but about the hinge inside of everything up to this point in the timeline. And I had just the one moment to look or look away, not enough time to ascertain what I knew. And so I relented. Held down in this chair in a kind of stoppage to balance something almost livable in that moment, that series of moments in the story that came before and after.

And so I shaped my answer into a yes.

I can still very clearly remember what the face of the district attorney looked like when I told what I'm not entirely sure was a lie.

I am so grateful to the friends who helped make me a better person during the production of this book. Thank you to Gillian Brecker, Brandon Brown, Melissa Catalano, CA Conrad, Lara Durback, Julian Hoeber, Phillip Andrew Lewis, Carmen Maria Machado, Jenn McCreary, Melissa Meader, Yedda Morrison, Anna Moschovakis, Daniel Fernández Pascual, Polly, Rosie, Jocelyn Saidenberg, Cassie Smith, Juliana Spahr, Syd Staiti, Alon Schwabe, Raina Trider, Carvell Wallace, Stephanie Young and Rachel Zolf.

Thank you to my writing group pals, including Megan Adams, Rebecca Bollinger, Gus, Pam Martin, Ron Palmer, Pony, Eric Sneathen, and Chet Weiner who listened along the way and helped muscle this book into shape.

Thank you Joel Gregory for your keen and thoughtful book design.

Thank you to Daniel Borzutzky, Kim Rosenfield and Trisha Low for your brilliant generosity.

Thank you Krupskaya for believing in this work and for navigating my every emotion in the process of making it a book. I could not ask for a smarter, kinder, funnier and lovelier team of champions. Thank you for continuing to put such stunning projects in the world and including mine in the heap.

Thank you to Frank, for always sitting at the table with me.

Thank you to Jonas. Even more than homicidal rabbits.